W9-CDX-704

Pilgrims

Written by Nicola Barber
Illustrated by David McAllister

p

This is a Parragon Publishing Book
First published in 2000

Parragon Publishing
Queen Street House
4 Queen Street
Bath BA1 1HE, UK

ISBN 0-75254-647-3

Printed in Singapore

Produced by
Monkey Puzzle Media Ltd
Gissing's Farm
Fressingfield
Suffolk IP21 5SH
UK

Designer: Sarah Crouch
Cover design: Victoria Webb
Editor: Linda Sonntag
Editorial assistance: Lynda Lines and Eileen Ramchandran
Indexer: Caroline Hamilton
Artwork commissioning: Roger Goddard-Coote
Project manager: Alex Edmonds

Contents

This Iroquois warrior carries a ball-headed club as part of his ceremonial war dress.

Who was there, before the Pilgrims came?

THE ALGONQUIN AND THE IROQUOIS WERE NATIVE AMERICAN TRIBES WHO LIVED IN NORTHEASTERN America. The Algonquin tribes spoke the Algonquian language and they included the Abenaki, Mahican, Narragansett, Pequot, and Wampanoag. They lived mainly along the coast. The Iroquois tribes spoke the Iroquoian language. They were based inland from the Algonquin tribes—around the St. Lawrence valley and the Great Lakes.

The beads that made up a wampum belt were also a form of currency.

What is a wampum?

A WAMPUM IS A BELT OF STRUNG BEADS MADE FROM WHELK AND CLAM shells. Wampum belts were valuable and sacred objects. They were exchanged as pledges of honor in political agreements between tribes. They were also worn at important occasions, such as weddings.

Who spoke of moccasins and tomahawks?
When Europeans started to settle in northeastern America, they soon came into contact with the local peoples and learned how to communicate with them. Some words of the Algonquian language eventually became so familiar that today they are part of the English language. They include "moccasin," "moose," and "tomahawk."

What was a sachem?
Sachem was the name given by tribes of the Northeast to their leaders. The five tribes of the Iroquois League elected 50 sachems who formed the governing body of the League.

Who were the people of the longhouse?
By the early 1600s, five of the Iroquoian-speaking tribes—the Cayuga, Mohawk, Oneida, Onondoga, and Seneca—had joined together to form the Iroquois League. They called themselves the "people of the longhouse." The League was a powerful alliance in warfare, and defeated the Huron, another Iroquoian-speaking tribe, in 1649.

Who shaved their heads?
In the Northeast, Native American men often shaved most of the hair off their heads, leaving only a small tuft on top. Another style was to shave only one side of the head, painting the shaven side. Women grew their hair to full length and wore it in single or double plaits down the back.

Who lived in wigwams?
Many of the tribes in the Northeast lived in cone- or dome-shaped tepees, often covered with birchbark. But the Iroquois made large rectangular homes called longhouses. They were built of elm poles covered with bark, and they could be up to 32 ft (10 m) long. Several related families lived in a longhouse, each family with its own sleeping area. An Iroquois village usually had several longhouses, surrounded by a tall fence, named a palisade, for security.

How did they catch fish?
The Native Americans of the Northeast ate a lot of fish, which they caught off the coast and in rivers and lakes. They made small fishing boats from hollowed-out tree trunks, or canoes from birch frames covered in bark. To trap fish, they used nets, spears, and fishing lines with bone hooks.

Who grew squashes and sunflowers?
Tribes of the Northeast cleared small areas of land to grow crops such as corn, squashes, sunflowers, and beans. Corn was a very important food, eaten all year round. The women planted and looked after the crops, and gathered nuts and berries from the forest.

Their greene corne

Corne newly sprong

Their sitting at meate

SECOTON

What did John White draw?

ONE OF THE MEMBERS OF THE EXPEDITION TO ROANOKE ISLAND in 1585 was an artist named John White. He made lots of sketches and watercolors of the animals and plants that he saw there, as well as the Native Americans he met.

What riches did Cabot find by the basketful?
Cabot did not bring back exotic spices and fabulous jewels from his voyage of 1497. But he did bring news of waters teeming with fish off the coast of Newfoundland—there were so many fish in the sea that they could be caught by lowering baskets weighted with stones over the side of the ship. Soon, fishermen from England, France, Italy, Portugal, and Spain were visiting these waters and coming home with huge loads of fish.

John White's illustrations showed what Native American life was like in the 1500s.

Who "found" Newfoundland?
The first known voyage across the Atlantic Ocean from Europe to North America was made by an Italian sailor called John Cabot in 1497. His ship was the *Matthew*, and his voyage was paid for by the English king, Henry VII. Like Christopher Columbus before him, Cabot thought that he was sailing to Asia —the land of spices and riches. Cabot did not find any riches, but he did make a landing, probably somewhere in present-day Newfoundland. Nearly a century later, in 1583, Sir Humphrey Gilbert sailed across the Atlantic on behalf of Queen Elizabeth I and claimed Newfoundland as an English territory.

Who were the first settlers to spend a winter in the New World?

In April 1585, a small fleet of five large and two smaller ships left England under the command of Richard Grenville. This expedition had been organized by Sir Walter Raleigh. Its aim was to set up a base for English warships at Roanoke Island (in present-day North Carolina). But the waters around the island were found to be too shallow for warships and, after one winter on the island, the colonists returned to England.

What was the message carved on the tree?

WHEN JOHN WHITE ARRIVED ON ROANOKE ISLAND IN 1590 TO LOOK FOR the colonists, the only clue he found was the word CROATOAN carved on a post. The Croatoan were Native Americans known to be friendly toward European settlers. They lived on a neighboring island. But storms stopped White from getting to their island, and the fate of the missing settlers was never known.

The Iroquois were based around the Great Lakes and lived in longhouses like these.

What happened to the "Lost Colony"?

In 1587, Sir Walter Raleigh organized a second expedition of colonists. This settlement was supposed to be on the mainland in the Chesapeake area—but the crossing took longer than expected and the captain refused to sail farther than Roanoke Island, where the colonists landed. The war between England and Spain and the Spanish Armada (1588) prevented any further voyages until 1590, when the artist John White sailed once again to Roanoke to join the colonists. But they had disappeared, and no trace of them was ever found.

What did the fishermen bring back apart from fish?

As the fishermen working along the coast of North America met up with the local peoples, a new trade began to develop. The Native Americans gave the fishermen furs to take back to Europe, in exchange for glass beads, cloth for clothes, and blankets, and iron tools.

Where did Jacques Cartier sail to?

Jacques Cartier was a sailor who came from St. Malo in France. Backed by the French king, Francis I, he made two expeditions in 1534 and 1535. He explored the Gulf of St Lawrence and the St. Lawrence River as far as modern-day Montreal.

Who founded Quebec?

In 1608, a group of French explorers led by Samuel de Champlain sailed to North America and made their way up the St. Lawrence River. They set up a fur trading post and named it Quebec. Only eight of the 24 colonists who founded Quebec were alive after the first winter in the new settlement, but Quebec itself survived and became the first settlement of New France.

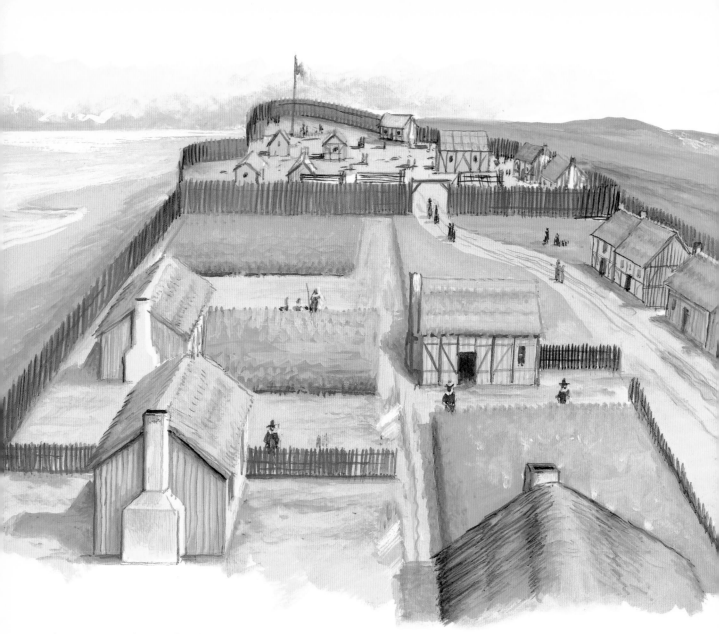

Jamestown was the site of the first successful British settlement in America.

Why was food scarce?

THE JAMESTOWN SETTLERS OFTEN ARGUED AMONG THEMSELVES ABOUT the running of the colony. As the first winter drew in, they realized that they had not grown enough crops to eat. This was mainly because so many men had deserted the fields to look for gold. The colony would not have survived its first winter without food from the Powhatans.

What treasure did English adventurers hope to find in the New World?

Gold! In the reign of Queen Elizabeth I, many great English captains roamed the seas. Sir Francis Drake was the first Englishman to sail around the world. Sir Walter Raleigh was the first to organize colonies of settlers in America. These captains were privateers—with the permission of their queen, they attacked and looted enemy ships, returning in triumph with their plunder. They also returned with wild tales of untold riches and of a city dripping with gold—El Dorado. These stories inspired many adventurers to try their luck in the New World.

Where did three ships find a permanent home?

After a journey across the Atlantic Ocean lasting about four months, 105 men in three ships sailed up the James River in Virginia and looked for somewhere to land. The year was 1607. Their ships were owned by the London Company, and their task was to find a natural harbor that would be safe from attack by England's enemy, the Spanish. When they found a good place, the adventurers began building simple shelters there. They called their new settlement Jamestown. It was the first permanent English settlement in North America.

Who were the Jamestown adventurers?

The men who sailed across the ocean to settle Jamestown were a mixed bunch. They included soldiers, labourers, craftsmen, a doctor, a priest, and several well-off gentlemen. Most hoped to make their fortunes in the New World, and they started to explore the area, searching for gold and other treasure.

How many settlers survived the first winter?

Out of the 105 settlers who landed in April 1607, only 35 were still alive after the first winter in the colony. Many died from diseases such as typhoid, malaria, and dysentery, others from starvation. Only the arrival of more settlers in 1608 and 1609 saved the colony from dying out.

Did the Native Americans help the settlers?

The Native Americans of the area were Algonquian-speakers led by a chief named Powhatan. At first the Powhatans were suspicious, but they were soon helping the settlers with supplies of food. Later, when the Powhatans realized that the newcomers intended to stay and take over their land, they attacked the colony, burning crops and killing livestock.

Who was John Smith?

After the disastrous first winter, it took a strong man to pull the colony through the following year. This man was a soldier named John Smith. He ruled with an iron fist, forcing the settlers to plant crops, and build houses and defenses.

Why did the settlers grow tobacco?

The colonists did not find gold, but they did discover a crop that grew well in Virginia, which they could sell in England for a profit. This crop was tobacco. In 1612 a settler called John Rolfe brought the first tobacco plants from the Caribbean, and two years later the first shipload of leaves was sent back to England from America.

Ætatis suæ 21. Aᵒ 1616.

Pocahontas became a Christian and changed her name to Rebecca when she married John Rolfe.

What happened to Pocahontas?

IN 1613, ONE OF THE DAUGHTERS OF CHIEF POWHATAN, NAMED POCAHONTAS, WAS KIDNAPPED BY THE COLONISTS. WHILE SHE was held captive, Pocahontas and the tobacco farmer John Rolfe fell in love, and the pair got married. This was the first marriage between a settler and a Native American, and it helped to make relations between the two sides more friendly.

Pilgrims believed that devotion to God could only be shown through worship, not through the clothes they wore. Pilgrims dressed very simply.

Who were the Pilgrims?

In November 1620, a group of men, women, and children made landfall on the rocky coastline of New England. Like the first settlers of Jamestown, these people had come to start a new life in the New World—but the reasons for their voyage were very different. They were not searching for gold, but for the freedom to follow their religion without persecution. They were called the Pilgrim Fathers.

What was a Nonconformist?

In the late 1500s and early 1600s, some people broke away from the Catholic and Anglican Churches. Because they did not conform to the established religions, they were called Nonconformists. They did not like the pomp and ceremony of church services, and did not believe that you needed a priest to help you talk to God. Instead, they worshipped solemnly in simple surroundings. There were many different Nonconformist groups, including the Pilgrims, the Puritans, and the Separatists.

What is Scrooby?

Scrooby, a small village in Nottinghamshire, England, was the center of the Nonconformist Church of the Pilgrims. Several Pilgrim leaders came from Scrooby, including John Robinson, William Brewster, and William Bradford.

How were Pilgrim children different?

THE PILGRIMS DISAPPROVED OF THE RELAXED WAY DUTCH CHILDREN WERE BROUGHT UP. DUTCH CHILDREN HAD FREEDOM to play, but the children of Pilgrim families were treated very strictly. They had to dress in dull clothes, and generally be seen and not heard.

Why did the Pilgrims flee to the Netherlands?

IN 1608, A GROUP OF NONCONFORMISTS FLED TO THE NETHERLANDS TO ESCAPE persecution in England. This was a risky business because the punishment for illegal emigration was prison. But the reward once they reached the Netherlands was great—freedom to worship as they wanted.

Why did the women and children get left behind?

The first attempt by the Pilgrims to flee to the Netherlands was led by William Brewster and John Robinson, in 1607. But the Pilgrims were robbed by the unscrupulous captain of the ship. A year later they tried again. This time the men went aboard the ship to check that there was no trap—only to watch their women and children being rounded up by the authorities on shore. The men had to sail without their families, and it was many months before they were reunited in the Netherlands.

Many Pilgrim women were expert weavers.

Why did the Pilgrims become weavers?

At first, the Pilgrims lived in the capital of the Netherlands, Amsterdam. But after a short time, they moved to the university town of Leiden, where many of them got jobs as weavers.

What was the Pilgrim Press?

It was a printing machine set up in Leiden by William Brewster. It was used to print pamphlets about the Nonconformist Church. These pamphlets were distributed in the Netherlands and, illegally, in England.

Why did the Pilgrims decide to leave the Netherlands?

The Pilgrims did not feel at home in the Netherlands. They did not want to follow a Dutch way of life or learn the Dutch language. Many Pilgrims began to talk about going to America—carving out a new life in an entirely new land.

How many people sailed on the Mayflower?

The second ship that the Pilgrims chose for their voyage to the New World was called the *Mayflower*. In 1620, it sailed from London to Southhampton, where it met up with the *Speedwell*. The two ships set sail together for the New World in August 1620, but were forced to turn back because the *Speedwell* was leaking very badly. A second attempt also failed, and the ships were forced to dock in Plymouth. The Pilgrims decided to abandon the *Speedwell*, and they all crowded onto the *Mayflower*. The *Mayflower* left Plymouth, England, on September 6, 1620.

Did the *Speedwell* speed well?

No! Once the Pilgrims had decided to sail across the Atlantic Ocean to the New World, their leaders looked for a ship to carry them from the Netherlands to England, and from there to their new home. They bought a small ship called the *Speedwell*, and had it fitted out to carry as many people as possible. The *Speedwell* made the short voyage to England without mishap, but it soon became clear that it was dangerously unseaworthy.

Was the crossing a good one?

No! It took 64 days from when the *Mayflower* sailed out of Plymouth harbor in England until land was sighted in the New World. The voyage was rough and stormy, and at one point it looked as if the ship might break apart. The wretched Pilgrims were thrown about helplessly in their cramped quarters, and many were continually seasick.

What did the Pilgrims take with them?

The Pilgrims were going to start a new life in the New World, so they packed as much as they could into the *Mayflower's* bursting holds. They took tools and equipment, as well as seeds and livestock. Many families took their dogs. They also needed to provide for themselves while at sea, so each family had its own bedding and cooking equipment.

Who kept a journal of the voyage?

One of the organizers of the expedition to the New World was a man named William Bradford. He wrote a journal recording the adventures of the Pilgrims on the crossing. He also listed every man, woman, and child aboard the *Mayflower*. From his list we know that there were 24 households as well as some single men. Bradford later became governor of the Pilgrims' new settlement.

The *Mayflower* was a
three-masted
carrack ship.

How big was the Mayflower?

THE *MAYFLOWER* WAS A SMALL SHIP TO FACE THE DANGERS OF AN ATLANTIC crossing. It was about 29 ft (9m) long, with a weight of about 180 tons. With 102 passengers aboard, as well as the ship's crew, and all their belongings, conditions were extremely cramped.

Why could the Pilgrims not land when they reached the shore?

When the excited Pilgrims saw land, they were desperate to get out of their damp and dirty quarters and onto dry land. But it was many days before the ship's captain could find a safe place to drop anchor. The Pilgrims first set foot in America at Cape Cod, in what is today Provincetown, Massachusetts.

What happened to the *Mayflower*?

The master of the *Mayflower*, Captain Jones, and his crew spent the first winter in the Pilgrims' new colony. It was not until the following April (1621) that the *Mayflower* set off on its return journey to England. It reached London in May, bringing the first news of the Pilgrims' safe arrival to friends and relations back home.

What other names were given to the Pilgrim Fathers?

The people who arrived in America on the *Mayflower* are also known as the "Forefathers," the "First Comers," and the "Old Stock."

How did a shallop help find a place to settle?

After signing the Mayflower Compact, a group of men went ashore to collect firewood and find a spring with fresh drinking water. Meanwhile, on board ship, the crew and some Pilgrims began to put together the small boat, named a shallop, that had been brought for exploring the coastline. It took many days to rebuild the shallop, but when it was ready, the Pilgrims took it in turns to set out in the shallop to look for a place to settle. They finally found somewhere with a safe harbor, several freshwater streams, and some abandoned fields. They called the place New Plymouth.

How did the Pilgrims celebrate that Christmas?

The Pilgrims arrived at their new home in the middle of winter. First they needed to build some kind of shelter so that families, stores, and equipment could be moved off the *Mayflower*. They spent Christmas Eve in prayer, but on Christmas Day it was business as usual—felling trees and cutting logs for building materials.

Why were the fields deserted?

The Pilgrims settled on a site that had been cleared and farmed by people before. But the fields were deserted. The Pilgrims learned later that an epidemic had killed most of the Native American inhabitants of this settlement, known as Patuxet, just two years earlier.

Who was the first governor of the colony?

After signing the Mayflower Compact, the Pilgrims elected a governor for their new colony. His name was John Carver, and he was so well-liked and respected that he was reelected in March 1621. Sadly, he died only a few weeks later, one of the last victims of the epidemic that claimed many Pilgrims' lives.

What argument ended in a compact?

As the *MAYFLOWER* sailed up and down the coastline of Cape Cod looking for somewhere to land, the Pilgrims on board started arguing. Some simply wanted to get off the ship, no matter where; others wanted to sail on and look for a really good landing place, close to other settlements. Some of the Pilgrims threatened to break from the group and set out alone, but in the end they agreed it would be better to stay together, and they all drew up a document laying down the laws and aims of the new colony. This document has became known as the Mayflower Compact. It was signed on board the *Mayflower* by 41 of the male Pilgrims on November 21, 1620.

How many Pilgrims survived the first winter?

After the rough ocean crossing, many of the Pilgrims were weak and in poor health when they arrived in the New World. Life was hardly any easier once they made landfall. In these appalling conditions, many of the Pilgrims fell ill, and during the first winter nearly half the group perished.

The Plymouth colony named their new settlement after the English town they sailed from.

When did the Pilgrims found New Plymouth?

A SMALL EXPEDITION OF PILGRIMS DECIDED ON THE SITE OF NEW Plymouth on December 21, 1620. They returned to the *Mayflower* in the shallop with the good news, and a few days later everything was prepared for the final stage of the *Mayflower*'s journey—a distance of about 24 miles (40 km).

As the pilgrims had no royal charter, they established government by signing the Mayflower Compact.

What happened to Dorothy Bradford?

Dorothy was the wife of William Bradford, who became governor of the colony after John Carver. She was one of the many Pilgrims to die in that first harsh winter. She was swept away by a sudden wave that broke over her as she stepped from the *Mayflower* into the waiting shallop below.

Did anyone give up and go home with the *Mayflower*?

No. Amazingly, despite the hardships of the winter, the surviving Pilgrims were determined to stay in the new colony, and none returned with the *Mayflower* when it departed for England in April 1621.

Initially the pilgrims and the Native Americans shared the land in harmony.

What did Samoset tell the Pilgrims?

SAMOSET HAD SPENT SOME TIME WITH THE EUROPEANS WHO FISHED ALONG THE coast, and knew enough phrases to be able to communicate with the Pilgrims. He told them about the geography of the coast to the north of New Plymouth, and that the place where they had settled had once belonged to the Patuxet tribe.

Who surprised the Pilgrims?

All that first winter, the Pilgrims were uneasily aware of the presence of Native Americans all around them. But, beset by sickness and the need to build shelter and hunt and fish for food, the settlers had little time to build defenses against any possible attack from hostile people. Then in mid-March, as the Pilgrims were holding a meeting to discuss how to defend themselves, a Native American strode into their settlement. His name was Samoset, and he was the Sagamore (chief) of the Morattigan tribe. This was the Pilgrims' first contact with the local people of the area.

How did some stolen corn save the colony?

The small groups of Pilgrims who left the *Mayflower* to search for a suitable landing place came across many signs of the Native Americans who had lived there. They unearthed some graves, filled with precious objects, which they quickly covered over again. They also found Native American stores full of corn. The Pilgrims knew that they needed all the food they could get for the winter, so they helped themselves to as much corn as they could carry. In fact, the stolen corn provided them with seed to plant the following spring and, without it, the new colony would probably not have survived.

How did the Native Americans help the Pilgrims?

THE NATIVE AMERICANS HAD LIVED OFF THE LAND FOR MANY CENTURIES, AND they were generous with their advice to the Pilgrims. They showed them how to plant the corn they had taken from an abandoned store the previous winter, and taught them new ways of cooking, farming and fishing.

What was Squanto's story?

Another Native American who spoke English was Squanto. He was from the Patuxet tribe, but had been kidnapped by the adventurer Captain Hunt and taken to London as a slave. He had managed to escape and return home. Squanto gave invaluable help to the Pilgrims, acting as an interpreter between them and the local Native Americans.

Who drew up a peace treaty?

The most important negotiations in the early days of the colony were held between Governor John Carver and the Sagamore (chief) of the Wampanoag tribe, whose name was Massasoit. With the help of the interpreter, Squanto, Carver and Massasoit drew up a peace treaty. The Pilgrims provided meat and brandy for the chief. In return, Massasoit gave them tobacco.

What was Samoset's warning?

Samoset warned the Pilgrims to beware of the Nauset tribe, who lived to the northeast of New Plymouth. The Nausets had reason to be hostile to Europeans, for only recently an English adventurer named Thomas Hunt had kidnapped several Nausets and Patuxets and taken them off to be sold as slaves.

Without advice from the Native Americans, the settlers would not have survived.

What was a house-raising?

WHEN THEY FIRST ARRIVED IN THE NEW WORLD, THE SETTLERS BUILT SHELTERS as quickly as possible from whatever materials came to hand. These simple homes were often made from wattles (woven frames) and sticks, plastered over with mud. The roofs were thatched with grass. But once a settlement was established, the colonists started to build more permanent houses. These were made of wood, and several families would work together to help with sawing tree trunks and setting heavy timbers into the ground. "House-raising" soon became a community occasion, when the owner would provide food and drink for the other settlers who came to help.

Why were the colonists afraid of the forests?

The first settlers in the New World were amazed at the thick forest that covered much of the land. It was easy to get lost in these forests, and the colonists were always fearful of attack from hostile Native Americans. So, at first, they avoided going into the woods as much as possible. Later, they used the forests as a valuable source of timber and game.

What do we remember at Thanksgiving today?

In the U.S. and Canada, Thanksgiving is celebrated every year, to remember the Pilgrims' first harvest. In the U.S. it is celebrated on the fourth Thursday of every November; in Canada the second Monday of October.

As the settlers grew used to their surroundings, they were able to build better homes that afforded them more protection.

Who planted fish?

The early settlers noticed that near rivers or the ocean, the Native Americans would place dead fish beneath their corn plants in the spring. They realized that the fish acted as a natural fertilizer, making the corn grow strongly. So the settlers followed the Native Americans' example.

Which crops did the settlers grow?

The first settlers who came to the New World from Europe brought with them seeds of the crops they grew at home, such as wheat. But they found that one of the best crops for the soil and climate of the Northeast was the corn grown by the Native Americans, and this became an important crop for the colonists.

Was the New World a land of plenty?

Yes! There were fish in the ocean and rivers, many wild berries and plants that were good for eating, and large quantities of game such as deer, ducks, and geese. There was also shellfish, such as oysters and clams, along the seashore.

Thanksgiving began as a celebration of the first harvest.

Who carried boats on their heads?

One of the easiest ways to get around in the New World was by water, along the great rivers that flowed into the Atlantic Ocean. The colonists copied the way the Native Americans made their canoes—from long strips of birchbark—to make light craft that could easily be carried around rapids or waterfalls.

Who ate the passenger?

The colonists were astonished by the numbers of pigeons that flew in the skies of the New World. These birds were passenger pigeons, and their huge flocks sometimes blacked out the entire sky. They were very easy to catch for food—so easy that the last passenger pigeon was killed in the 1800s and the bird is now extinct.

Who ate five deer at Thanksgiving?

IN THE AUTUMN OF 1621, THE PILGRIMS HARVESTED THEIR FIRST CROPS IN THE New World. In the spring they had planted barley, peas, and the Native American corn. The corn had grown well, although the barley and peas were less successful. The Pilgrims held a feast to give thanks for this store of food, which was enough to see them through the winter. Sagamore Massasoit and about 90 of his tribe came to share the Pilgrims' feast, bringing five deer with them. This was the first Thanksgiving.

How many more Pilgrim Fathers came to Plymouth?

IN THE YEARS THAT FOLLOWED, TWO MORE SHIPS ARRIVED WITH PILGRIM settlers from the Netherlands and England. In 1623, the *Anne* sailed into Plymouth harbor carrying about 60 Pilgrims. A few days later, a small ship called the *Little James* also arrived, for the Pilgrims to use for trade along the coast of North America. Finally, in 1630, the *Handmaid* brought another 60 Pilgrims. These were the last arrivals to be able to call themselves the "Pilgrim Fathers of New England."

New arrivals landing at Plymouth without supplies placed an extra strain on already limited food supplies.

What did *Fortune* bring in 1621?

The Pilgrims had lived in the New World for one year, when an unexpected arrival took the small colony by surprise. On November 21, 1621, a ship sailed into Plymouth harbor. Fearing that it might be an enemy ship, the Pilgrims ran to grab their weapons —but it was the *Fortune* carrying a second wave of colonists. Joyfully, the Pilgrims ran to the shore to greet the new arrivals.

What good news did the *Fortune* bring?

The *Fortune* brought news and letters from friends and family at home—the first communication with the outside world since the Pilgrims had arrived in the New World.

...and what about the bad news?

The Pilgrims' expedition on the *Fortune* had been very badly planned. There was barely enough food on board to keep the new settlers alive during the crossing. To the horror of the original colonists in Plymouth, the new settlers had brought no supplies or equipment with them. The number of extra mouths to feed brought the colony close to starvation over that winter.

Who got ambushed by pirates?

The colonists loaded the *Fortune* with trade goods to be sold in England—beaver skins and roughly sawn timber. The ship set sail on December 21, 1621, but on its return journey across the Atlantic, it was captured by French pirates. They stole the Pilgrims' precious cargo and delayed the arrival of their letters in England.

Who came unprepared?

Two shiploads of adventurers from England arrived in 1622, just as the settlers were close to starvation. The new arrivals brought no supplies with them, and relied on the Pilgrims' goodwill and hospitality. When the newcomers finally left to set up their own colony, they left their sick behind for the Pilgrims to nurse back to health.

Who was brought back to life?

One day, word came to the Pilgrims that Massasoit, the Sagamore (chief) of the local Native Americans, was dying. Massasoit had been a good friend to the Pilgrims, so Governor Bradford decided to send him medicine. And after drinking the herbal remedies prepared by the Pilgrims, the Sagamore recovered.

Massasoit's statue is a tribute to the Native Americans who supported the Pilgrims during very difficult times.

What happened to the Pilgrims?

The Pilgrims survived Native American attack, starvation, and illness and their colony survived. As more settlers arrived in New England, trade increased and the Pilgrims became more prosperous. But their colony remained small and in the 1690s it was taken over by the larger and more powerful colony of Massachusetts.

What was Massasoit's warning?

To thank the Pilgrims for their help, Massasoit warned them about a planned raid. He had forbidden his own tribe to take part, but he knew that other tribes were about to attack Plymouth and a neighboring settlement set up by the English adventurers.

Like other Nonconformists, Quakers were persecuted for their beliefs.

What was the largest expedition to the New World?

In March 1630, a fleet of 11 ships left England for America. On board were nearly 1,000 men, women, and children. This massive expedition was organized by the Massachusetts Bay Company, and its leader was John Winthrop, a Puritan landowner from Suffolk in the east of England. Even before he sailed on the *Arabella*, Winthrop had been elected governor of the new colony. When they arrived in the New World, the settlers chose a site near the Charles River. They called it Boston, after the town in Lincolnshire, England, where many of them had lived.

Why did New Amsterdam become New York?

English settlers were not the only European colonizers arriving in the New World. In 1625, a small group of settlers from the Netherlands set up a trading post on Manhattan Island, calling it New Amsterdam. The colonists found that the land on Manhattan was suitable for growing crops, and the settlement flourished. Then in 1664, the Dutch colony was attacked and captured by English forces, and its name was changed—to New York, after the town of York, in England.

Were the Puritans well prepared?

Yes. The Puritan settlers had learned what to bring with them from the letters written back home by the Pilgrims. They crammed their ships full of tools and equipment, as well as livestock. Within a very short time, they had set up 11 towns around the Boston area.

Who were the Puritans?

THE PURITANS WERE NONCONFORMISTS WHO DISAPPROVED OF THE ANGLICAN Church. They dressed soberly in simple clothes, and they led a pure life without entertainment. In the new colonies, Governor Winthrop banned theatrical performances and drinking. But everyone had to go to church.

How many more settlers arrived?

John Winthrop's expedition of 1630 was followed by many ships full of settlers from England. Over the next 10 years, thousands more people arrived in America to settle in New England. Many of them were Puritans, or sympathetic to the Puritan way of life.

How many families were needed to start a town?

Towns grew up amazingly quickly as more and more settlers arrived in Massachusetts. A group of about 20 families would join together to found a new town. Once they had been granted land, they laid out a village street with a simple church at its center. A plot of land next to the church was reserved for the minister to build a house. Then areas of about one acre were marked out for the other homes.

Did everyone follow the Puritan way of life?

N O! MANY SETTLERS WERE NOT PURITANS AND DID NOT LIKE THE PURITAN way of life. Some of these people formed breakaway colonies. Rhode Island was founded by Roger Williams, who had been banished from the Massachusetts colony for disagreeing with its leaders.

Who named a colony after the Virgin Mary?

The Pilgrims were not the only people to suffer religious persecution in England. When King Henry VIII set up the Anglican Church in the 1500s, Roman Catholics were prevented from worshipping as they wanted. In 1633, two ships sailed for America carrying Catholic settlers. They founded a colony and called it Maryland.

Who were the Quakers?

The Quakers were a group of English Nonconformists who followed the teaching of a preacher called George Fox. In the early 1680s, a group of Quakers organized by William Penn set sail for America. They were the first settlers in the State of Pennsylvania.

A New England kitchen contained objects brought from Europe as well as newly-crafted utensils.

Why were fish and furs important?

The early settlers discovered that their new home was rich in two valuable natural resources—fish and furs. In fact, fishermen had long known about the plentiful supplies of fish in the North Atlantic Ocean. Fur traders were often the first adventurers to explore new areas, far in advance of any settlers. Most traders bartered with the local Native Americans, who were skilled trappers, for the hides of deer, moose, bear, otter, and beaver.

What did La Salle find downriver?

After Champlain founded Quebec and New France, the land that is present-day Canada was crossed and re-crossed by adventurers in pursuit of furs. Many of these adventurers were French, and gradually they explored the area from Hudson Bay to the Great Lakes. Some pushed even farther south. From 1679 to 1682 the French explorer René Robert Cavalier de La Salle made an epic journey down the Mississippi River as far as the Gulf of Mexico, claiming a vast area of land, Louisiana, for the French crown.

Why was the Hudson's Bay Company set up?

The Hudson's Bay Company was set up in 1670 by English fur traders. English and French traders competed for control of the fur trade in the north, and quarrels often broke out between the two sides.

What was salt cod?

O F ALL THE FISH CAUGHT OFF THE COAST OF NEWFOUNDLAND, COD WAS THE MOST important. This was because it could be dried and cured with salt to stop it from going bad. The salt fish was then taken back to Europe and sold in ports such as La Rochelle on the Atlantic coast of France.

Fig. 3.

Cod fishing provided an income for many settlers.

What did the traders exchange for furs?

THE NATIVE AMERICANS PROVIDED THE VALUABLE SKINS TO THE FUR

traders in return for all sorts of goods including tools, guns, jewelry, pots, and pans, clothes, and blankets.

Who bought the furs?

Most of the furs were shipped back to Europe. They were used for clothing—for example, deerskin was used to make gloves. Some of the furs were sold in the growing colonies along the east coast where they were used to make coats and breeches (knee-length pants).

How did the trappers get about?

Trappers usually went by canoe. Most canoes were made from birchbark. There were lots of birch trees wherever the trappers went, so repairs were quick and easy. Resin, the sticky sap from trees, was used along the canoe seams to make them watertight.

How were whales caught?

Whaling expeditions set out in small rowing boats equipped with a harpoon. A harpoon was a spear with a long line attached to it. When the boat was close enough to the whale, the harpoon was thrust deep into its body and the line let out until the injured whale was exhausted. Whaling was a very dangerous way of making a living.

Furs from America fetched a good price in Europe.

How did wood produce metal?

The huge forests of northeastern America provided the settlers with a rich supply of timber for houses, shipbuilding, and barrel-making. Wood was also burned to make charcoal. The charcoal was exported to Europe, where it was used in the manufacture of iron and steel.

How did the colonists defend themselves?

ONE OF THE FIRST THINGS EUROPEAN SETTLERS DID WHEN THEY arrived in America was to protect themselves against possible Native American attack. So they spent a lot of time and effort building forts, and they set up armed forces, named militias. Captain Miles Standish was the leader of the Pilgrims' first militia.

As relations between Native Americans and settlers became strained, armed forces were set up in settlements.

Why did friendship turn to warfare?
At the start, settlers and Native Americans were often friendly to each other. The Native Americans helped the newcomers with supplies and know-how for their survival, as they struggled to set up their colonies. In return, the settlers gave them goods that they did not produce for themselves, such as pots and pans, knives, blankets, guns, and alcohol. But as the settlers took over more land and became more threatening, the Native Americans grew more hostile. Sometimes there was open warfare.

Who died in the massacres of 1622?
By 1622, the colony in Virginia had grown to cover an area over 100 miles (161 km) along the James River. The local Native Americans realized that they were losing their land and that their way of life was threatened. They attacked the colonists and massacred over 350 settlers. Many Native Americans died in the revenge attacks that followed.

Why did the Native Americans fall sick?
As more and more European settlers poured into America, the Native Americans who had lived there for generations began to suffer badly, and in many ways. Probably their worst enemy was both silent and invisible. European settlers brought illnesses with them that were entirely new to the Native Americans. They had no resistance to diseases such as smallpox. Thousands of Native Americans died as epidemics swept through their tribes in the 1600s.

How many died from European diseases?

It is very difficult to know exactly how many Native Americans were living in northeastern America before the arrival of the European settlers. Some historians believe that the area of New England was home to about 25,000 Native Americans in 1600. It is likely that more than half of this number died from disease in the 20 years after the first settlers arrived.

What was the Pequot War?

This was the first large-scale battle between Native Americans and settlers in the northeast. The Pequots had moved east, threatening both the local tribes and the European colonists. In 1637, the English settlers attacked the Pequots and wiped out almost the entire tribe.

Who wanted tribal warfare?

The European settlers knew that if the Native American tribes were busy fighting each other, they were less likely to attack the colonists. So, many colonies did their best to encourage bad feelings between tribes.

Who was shot in a swamp?

Chief Metacomet was finally cornered and shot in a swamp. King Philip's War was a disaster for the Native American population. Thousands died, leaving much of the coastal regions of northeast America clear for the Europeans to move into.

Who was King Philip?

AFTER THE DEATH OF MASSASOIT IN 1662, HIS SON METACOMET BECAME CHIEF. The colonists called him "Philip" or "King Philip." Because of the land they were taking from him, Metacomet was not as friendly to the settlers as his father. He led his people in a war against them that lasted from 1675 to 1676. This became known as King Philip's War.

King Philip enlisted the help of other Native American tribes in his struggle against the settlers.

Jefferson wrote part of the Declaration of Independence.

When was the Declaration of Independence?

THE AMERICAN COLONISTS DECLARED THEMSELVES INDEPENDENT FROM BRITAIN on July 4th, 1776. But the fighting went on until 1783 before Britain recognized the independence of the United States of America.

When did the first Africans arrive in North America?

Early settlers in Virginia set sail for Africa, returning with African captives to work on their plantations around 1619. This was the beginning of the terrible slave trade.

Who won the Seven Years' War?

Great Britain eventually won the war after seven long years. The capital of New France, Quebec, surrendered in 1760. By the end of the war in 1763, the British had taken over New France and governed the whole of eastern North America.

What were the 13 colonies?

Europeans continued to settle the northeast coast of America throughout the end of the 1600s and the beginning of the 1700s. By 1733, there were 13 British colonies in North America. They were Connecticut, Delaware, Georgia, Maine, Maryland, Massachusetts, New Hampshire, New Jersey, New York, Pennsylvania, Rhode Island, Vermont, and Virginia. They were all ruled by a government far away in Great Britain—but this situation was soon to change.

Who fought a war over furs?

Ever since the first trappers explored the waterways of northern America, the English and French had fought to control the fur trade, which was making them so much money. The two sides engaged in lots of small wars, often helped by their Native American allies. But the most bitter struggle began in 1754. The fighting spread to Europe in 1756, and lasted for seven years, until 1763. It became known as the Seven Years' War.

What started the American Revolution?

Which was the last of the 13 colonies to be founded?
Georgia. Its charter was issued in 1732, and the first settlers arrived from England in 1733.

DURING THE 1760S AND 1770S, THE GOVERNMENT IN BRITAIN imposed a series of taxes on the colonists in America. The colonists had no representatives in the British parliament and therefore no one to argue their cause. Finally, in 1775, the colonists' resentment boiled over into armed resistance. This was the beginning of the American Revolution.

Colonists became disillusioned with being governed by a far-off country that knew little about their lives.

Why did the British demand money from their colonies?
After the Seven Years' War the British colonists in America no longer feared a French invasion from the north. But the British government decided that their colonies needed a permanent army and navy—and they expected the colonies to pay toward the upkeep of these forces.

What happened at Bunker Hill?
The opening skirmishes of the American Revolution happened at Concord and nearby Lexington in April 1775. The first major battle was at Bunker Hill. The colonists were forced to flee, but not until they had killed or wounded more than 1,000 British soldiers.

The trail cut across the
Appalachians by Daniel Boone
and his 30 woodsmen became
known as the Wilderness Road. It
started in Virginia, crossed the
mountains at the Cumberland
Gap, and ended in Kentucky.

Where did Daniel Boone cut a trail?

THE SETTLERS IGNORED
THE BAN ON EXPLORING
west of the Appalachian Mountains. In
1775, a judge called Richard
Henderson bought a huge area of land
in Kentucky from the Cherokees. Then
he employed the pioneer Daniel
Boone to cut a trail through the
Appalachian Mountains to his land.
Boone had spent many years exploring
the mountains and beyond, and knew
the area better than any other white
man of the time.

Daniel Boone was captured by the
Shawnee during the American
Revolution, but escaped and reached
Boonesborough in time to save it
from the British.

Why did people go West?
To claim land. Thousands of
people from Europe continued to
pour into America. Between 1763
and 1776 alone, up to 150,000
people settled there. More people
needed more land, and the
government could do nothing to
stop them moving west to find it.

Where did Daniel Boone build a town?

At the end of the Wilderness Road, Boone and his companions built a settlement which they called Boonesborough. It was near the present-day town of Lexington. In a short time several families had settled around Boonesborough, including the owner of the territory, Judge Henderson.

Who trapped the trapper?

Boone met many Native Americans as he traveled through the mountains and beyond. Often, these meetings were hostile and Boone was taken prisoner. He was set free only after he had given up his few possessions and whatever furs he had managed to trap.

Who lost his homeland twice?

Boone lost his land in Kentucky because he could not prove his legal right to own it. In 1799, he led another group of settlers, this time into Missouri. Once again, he lost the land he had claimed. He died in Missouri in 1820.

Who drew a line at the Appalachian Mountains?

As the Seven Years' War came to an end and Britain took control of French land in North America, many Native American tribes began to rebel. These Native Americans had long been allies of the French, and they did not trust Great Britain. In 1763, after several ferocious battles between Native Americans and British troops, the British government ordered all settlers west of the Appalachian Mountains to withdraw to the east. It also forbade new settlement west of the mountains—the idea was to leave this area free for the Native Americans.

People living in frontier villages had to be entirely self-sufficient.

Who were the "back-woodsmen"?

THE PIONEERS CLEARED LAND IN THE KENTUCKY forests for their crops and built themselves rough houses from logs. They were known as "backwoodsmen"—farmers who needed to be entirely self-sufficient in order to survive.

Who followed Boone to the West?

For many years the Wilderness Road was the only practical route through the mountains to Kentucky. Despite its dangers, over 200,000 settlers had used the Wilderness Road to move west by 1800.

Index

ACKNOWLEDGEMENTS
The photographs in this book were supplied
by: Peter Newark's Pictures 4, 9, 13, 30; Photri
6, 11, 15, 18, 19, 20, 21, 23, 24, 27, 28.